Queen Elizabeth II

A Woman of Inestimable Value (End of an Era)

Williams George

TABLE OF CONTENT

INTRODUCTION

A seventy-year reign that started in the early nineteen-fifties, during Winston Churchill's second premiership, came to an end on Thursday (8th September 2022) in Scotland. Her son, now known as Charles III, will take her place. The passing of the Queen has sparked discussions on the worth of constitutional monarchy as well as a period of prolonged mourning in the UK and other parts of the world. The Queen's Platinum Jubilee, which commemorated 70 years of her service to the British Commonwealth, was celebrated in the UK in February 2022 with a number of events. Queen Elizabeth II demonstrated consistency and tenacity before passing away at the age of 96. She lost her 73-year marriage to Prince Phillip in April 2021 when he passed away at age 99. She appointed her fifteenth prime minister. Liz Truss, just two days before she passed away.

Chapter One
Early Life

Given that her father was a junior son of King George V, Elizabeth Alexandra Mary, the eldest daughter of Prince Albert, Duke of York and his wife, Lady Elizabeth Bowes-Lyon, was thought to have little prospect of succeeding to the throne when she was born on April 21, 1926.

To have the pleasure of marrying Wallis Simpson, a divorcee from the United States, her uncle King Edward VIII abdicated the throne in 1936. Following her father's coronation as King George VI, the 10-year-old was designated as the heir apparent to the throne.

Princess Elizabeth was greatly influenced by her mother, who instilled in her a devout Christian faith and a keen awareness of the demands of royal life, despite the fact that she spent a large portion of her childhood with nannies. Elizabeth and her younger sister Margaret received etiquette instruction from their grandmother, Queen Mary, consort of King George V.

The princess received a private education with a focus on British history and law, as well as lessons in music and fluent French. She obtained Girl Guide training, the British equivalent of Girl Scouts, and a lifetime love of horses.

She had a lot of thoroughbred racehorses as the queen, and she frequently went to races and breeding competitions. Elizabeth had a well-known bond with Pembroke Welsh corgis as a young kid and owned more than 30 of them during her reign.

Elizabeth and Margaret lived separated from their parents for a significant portion of World War II in the Royal Lodge at Windsor Castle, a fortified castle outside of London. The king elevated Elizabeth to the rank of honorary colonel in the Royal Army's 500 Grenadier Guards in 1942.

He appointed her to the Privy Council and the Council of State two years later, allowing her to represent him while he was away from the country.

Elizabeth's engagement to Prince Philip of Greece, a lieutenant in the Royal Navy and her third cousin (both were great-great-grandchildren of Queen Victoria and Prince Albert), was announced in 1947, not long after the royal family had returned from an official visit to South Africa and Rhodesia. When she was just 13, she had already set her sights on him, and over the course of the war, their relationship grew through visits and letters.

Princess Elizabeth traveled to South Africa at the beginning of 1947 with the king and queen. Following her return, news of her engagement to her distant cousin Lieutenant Philip Mountbatten of the Royal Navy—previously Prince Philip of Greece and Denmark—was made public.

Despite the fact that many people in the royal circle believed Philip and Elizabeth were a bad match due to his lack of riches and foreign origin, Elizabeth was steadfastly loyal and madly in love. She wed Philip on November 20, 1947, in Westminster Abbey.

Prince Charles (now King Charles iii), their first child, was born in 1948, and Anne (now Princess Royal), their second child, was born in 1950.

Elizabeth and Phillip have been married for an incredible 73 years before the Prince's dying in April 2021 at the age of 99.

Chapter Two
The Journey to Sovereignty

In 1951, as her father's health deteriorated, Elizabeth stood in for him at various public functions. Elizabeth and Philip spent that year's Christmas with the royal family before departing for a tour to Australia and New Zealand. They made a stop in Kenya on route.

King George VI, who was 56 years old, died of lung cancer on February 6, 1952, making his 25-year-old daughter the sixth woman to rule the United Kingdom. They were at the time in Kenya. In Westminster Abbey, she was solemnly crowned Queen Elizabeth II on June 2, 1953.

Elizabeth became accustomed to her role as queen during the first ten years of her reign, growing close to Prime Minister Winston Churchill (the first of 15 prime ministers she would work with during her reign), surviving the Suez Crisis of 1956, and taking numerous state trips abroad.

The queen adopted measures to modernize the monarchy's and her own image after receiving sharp criticism in the media, such as the first broadcast of her annual Christmas message on television in 1957.

Andrew, who was born in the year 1960, and Edward were Elizabeth and Philip's other two children (born 1964). After reaching adulthood and commencing a protracted spell as king-in-waiting, Charles was formally invested as the Prince of Wales in 1968.

In a time of economic hardship, Queen Elizabeth's Silver Jubilee in 1977—which celebrated her 25 years as monarch—served as a ray of hope. She was always a hard traveler, and to commemorate the event, she kept a punishing schedule that took her 56,000 miles across the Commonwealth, including the island nations of Fiji and Tonga, New Zealand, Australia, Papua New Guinea, the British West Indies, and Canada.

The family came back into the public eye in 1981 with the royal wedding of Prince Charles and Lady Diana Spencer at London's St. Paul's Cathedral. William and Harry, two sons, were soon welcomed into the world, but their marriage swiftly fell apart, humiliating the queen and the rest of the royal family in front of the public.

Princess Anne and her husband, Mark Phillips, separated in 1992, which Elizabeth referred to as the family's "Annus Horribilis" because it saw the split of Charles and Diana, Prince Andrew and his wife, Sarah Ferguson, and Prince Andrew and Princess Anne.

The Commonwealth

The love of the Queen was one of the factors that kept the Commonwealth united; now that she is gone and in light of the rise of nationalist and anti-colonial feeling in the former colonies, the Commonwealth's future is doubtful.

For the British Commonwealth, 14 of which still recognize Queen Elizabeth II as their Head of State—a status that is expressly expressed in the constitutions and statutes of some of these nations—the departure of the monarch is a sensitive time. If there is strong

resistance to the current status, it may be necessary in these situations to amend the law or statute, which could lead to calls for a referendum. One such instance is Jamaica, which has a good chance of leaving the Commonwealth after becoming a republic in 2021, like its Caribbean neighbor Barbados.
The political systems of developed nations with constitutional monarchies, such as Australia, New Zealand, and Canada, are set up so that the new monarch of the United Kingdom will become their head of state as part of the regular process. The appointment of Matt Thistlewaite as the nation's first minister to supervise the country's transition to a republic by Australia's new government, led by Prime Minister Anthony Albanese, in June, however, sparked speculation that a referendum to depose the Queen as head of state might follow.

56 nations make up the Commonwealth of Nations, or simply the Commonwealth, the vast majority of which were formerly British colonies. They are usually found in the Pacific, the Americas, Asia, and Africa. The Commonwealth is made up of three European countries: Malta, Cyprus, and the United Kingdom.

Together with the UK, 14 of these 56 nations make up the "Commonwealth realms". They are Solomon Islands, Tuvalu, Saint Kitts and Nevis, Saint Lucia, Saint Vincent and the Grenadines, Australia, Antigua and Barbuda, The

Bahamas, Belize, Canada, Grenada, Jamaica, and New Zealand. The head of state of these nations is the British monarch, now King Charles III, the eldest child of Queen Elizabeth II. 36 of the Commonwealth's remaining 41 members are republics, including Bangladesh, Sri Lanka, Pakistan, and India. Eswatini (formerly Swaziland), Tonga, Lesotho, Malaysia, and Brunei Darussalam all have their own monarchs.

The Commonwealth Games, an international multisport competition conducted every four years in one of the member nations, are the most obvious aspect of the Commonwealth that unites all of its nations. Even though there are more extensive aspects of intergovernmental cooperation within the grouping, the Commonwealth Games—which were hosted by India in 2010 and whose most recent edition was finished in Birmingham, England, last month—remain the only association that the average Indian makes with the organization.

One third of the world's population, or 2.5 billion people, call the Commonwealth home, with the majority of them residing in the Indian subcontinent. The lesser Commonwealth kingdoms are the final holdovers of Britain's colonial empire, tying the British monarch to around 150 million people living outside of the UK. Most current people of Commonwealth nations have never had a direct interaction with the British government. As aspirations for independence grew more powerful, Queen Victoria made an effort to preserve control over the colonies, which led to the creation of the Commonwealth. The Queen decided to grant the area dominion status in 1867 when Canada voiced its displeasure with imperial monitoring. This meant that the territory would have self-rule, but that Britain may veto measures at the monarch's discretion. Other British colonies—mostly white ones—like Australia, New Zealand, and South Africa also evolved into dominions in the next decades. Following World War I, rising nationalist waves in the dominions compelled further reforms, and in 1926, Britain and the dominions decided they would be on an equal footing. The British Commonwealth of Nations was formally established in 1931 as a result of this declaration, which was codified in the Statute of Westminster. Leaders of the Indian National Movement advocated for complete independence at those negotiations even if India was present. Prime Minister Jawaharlal Nehru accepted the invitation to join the Commonwealth in 1949 with a crucial proviso. India had just gained its independence. India requested that it be granted membership without having to make a Crown-allegiance oath. As a result of the member countries' agreement, Sri Lanka, Pakistan, and India joined the Commonwealth later that year.

Mozambique, Rwanda, Togo, and Gabon, four Commonwealth nations, have no historical ties to the

British Empire. Rwanda was governed by the Belgians and Germans, Togo and Gabon by the French, and Mozambique was a colony of the Portuguese.
On April 21, 1947, the late Queen's 21st birthday, she made a broadcast to the youth of the British family of nations in which she vowed to dedicate her life to the service of the union. This act solidified her commitment to the Commonwealth.

The Queen began a tour across the Commonwealth and was welcomed with great pomp and enthusiasm after her coronation on June 2, 1953 (she had ascended the throne on February 6, 1952, the day her father, King George VI, passed away). She traveled to well over a hundred nations during her lengthy reign, making her one of history's most traveled heads of state. Despite the fact that she rarely expressed her social opinions in public, her numerous trips became icons of Britain's diplomacy. Many of her excursions also put a strong emphasis on racial equality and international relations. She traveled to South Africa in 1995 to mark the end of apartheid and to welcome the country into the Commonwealth. Some have argued that the Queen needed the Commonwealth more than it needed her, including historians like Ben Pimlott. The monarchy, with its imperial memory, ardently sought a Commonwealth role, partly to justify itself but also because it had taken its supranational role seriously. In a way that was never quite understood by politicians, it continued to relate to distant communities that showed their loyalty in ways that did not necessarily come to the attention of Whitehall.

It is crucial to stress that the Queen had no influence over the administration of either the Commonwealth of Nations' member states or the Commonwealth realms, of which she served as head of state. She had various constitutional responsibilities in the latter set of nations, including approving new administrations and occasionally legislation, bestowing state honors, and appointing specific individuals.

But save from one notable exception, all of these functions were always primarily ceremonial. To end a legislative impasse in 1975, Sir John Kerr, the Governor General of Australia and the Queen's representative there, unilaterally fired Gough Whitlam, the Labour Party's then-prime minister, and appointed Malcolm Fraser, the leader of the opposition, to take his place. As a result, Australia experienced what has been called its worst constitutional crisis ever.

Numerous nations, including Dominica, Guyana, and Trinidad and Tobago, made the decision to quit the Commonwealth in the 1970s, thereby deposing the Queen as their head of state. The Governor General of Barbados stated that "the time has come fully to leave our colonial past behind" as the island nation exited the realm in 2021. The departure coincided with Barbados' 55th anniversary of being independent from the UK. Britain's interests could not coincide with those of the other member states, which is another justification for quitting. Those divisions have historically included foreign policy issues, even though they may now be mostly cultural. The Union of South Africa and Canada took longer to declare war on Nazi Germany in 1939 than the UK did. King George VI reigned as the monarch of the UK, SA, and CA at that time, and he had war and peace relations with Germany. Black Lives Matter protests have strained relations between the crown and its black Commonwealth subjects, which are uncommon in today's world of stark disparities. The realm's Jamaica was particularly outspoken in this regard, lobbying the Queen for compensation for the Crown's culpability in the transatlantic slave trade.

Analysts have questioned whether the new monarch, in the absence of Elizabeth, would be able to legally appoint Governors-General in Commonwealth nations if those nations did not first amend their constitutions to refer to the "King" as their head of state rather than the Queen.

A revision to Canada's constitution would be necessary if it decided to leave the realm. It would need to be a referendum in Australia's situation. The Australian Parliament was denied the right to choose the country's head of state in a referendum in 1999 by a vote of 45%

to 55%, but the current administration may call another one.

However, in the end, the Queen's enormous popularity and goodwill, which she enjoyed in both the UK and the Commonwealth, served as a unifying glue. The destiny of the Commonwealth may ultimately depend on whether Charles and Queen Consort Camilla are viewed with similar affection. In fact, it has been suggested that with the end of Elizabeth II's reign, a union that was fundamentally founded on subordination and is tarnished by its ties to racism and colonial tyranny should likewise be let to dissolve.

Chapter Three
Constitutional Powers of a British Monarch

Great Britain formally transitioned to a constitutional monarchy in 1689. This means that an elected body known as Parliament has the authority to enact laws.

Reserve powers, usually referred to as prerogative powers or personal prerogatives, were granted to Queen Elizabeth (and now King Charles).
The monarch, who guards the nation's Constitution, can utilize these rights to name and remove ministers, call sessions of Parliament, and grant royal assent to legislation approved by those bodies. Notably, even if a prime minister loses the support of the House of Commons, the king or queen can oust him or her. Despite the fact that those powers seem immense, they are qualified. Bills are presumed to have received the royal assent when they pass both Houses of Parliament, and the king is normally summoned on the recommendation of the ministers who make that recommendation.

Like his mother before him, King Charles III reigns rather than rules. The main distinction is that he is not permitted to issue decrees or anything even vaguely resembling an edict. Instead, he is seen as a symbol of appropriate decorum and grace.
The queen continues to serve as the official leader of both the military and the Church of England. The primary function of the monarch, as stated on the king's official website, royal.uk, is to carry out constitutional and representational obligations cultivated over 1,000 years of British history.

At her coronation in 1953, Queen Elizabeth, who found solace in her Christian religion, made an oath to uphold and protect inviolably the Church of England's settlement, as well as its doctrine, worship, discipline, and government, as prescribed by English law. Charles is anticipated to continue this custom. Elizabeth began addressing the General Synod, a gathering of Church of England officials, in 1970 and did so every five years for the remainder of her reign.
She also had a custom of giving cash to elderly on Maundy Thursday, the day when Christians remember Jesus' Last Supper. She performed this in cathedrals and churches all around the realm.

The ceremonial head of the British Armed Forces is the monarch or queen, to whose allegiance is sworn by military personnel, many of whom over the years have been members of the House of Windsor.
However, the power to actually use armed forces is shifted from the sovereign to the prime minister and secretary of defense, who then, similarly to the U.S. Presidential system of government, delegate such duties to career officers. Although the king had extensive power in the past, elected officials currently have that authority. Today, a monarch could issue proclamations of war and peace, but only with the approval of the executive.
The Elizabeth Cross, granted to families of those murdered as a result of military operations or terrorism,

will certainly continue to be presented by King Charles III, who served in the Royal Air Force and the Royal Navy in the 1970s. He will undoubtedly be present for many military parades and festivities.

The monarchy saw considerable changes during Queen Elizabeth's 70-year reign. King Charles may want to further tone back affairs, possibly limiting important engagements to himself and the heir apparent, Prince William, experts say, as a result of personal scandals and a growing mood that questions the purpose of a monarchy.

There are other privileges a British Monarch enjoys. The British Monarch King Charles III needs no driving license to make his legal moves; He also needs no license plate or number plate while making his travels. He is arguably the only personality in the world that drives legally without any license issuance. Unlike other Royal Families, the King himself doesn't need any UK Passport before embarking on any International travels as the UK's Passport will now bear his identity.

The King together with other members of the Royal Family is exclusively entitled to the service of a Private Cash Machine (ATM) which is installed at the Buckingham Palace. A British Monarch doesn't vote and he (King Charles III) is expected to remain extremely neutral in political matters. Being a Monarch, he cannot be arrested nor charged to court.

Chapter Four
Celebrations and Anniversaries

An extraordinary number of significant events have occurred during the reign of the Queen. In the extraordinary years that have passed since her Accession, Her Majesty's birthdays and jubilees have served as an occasion for contemplation and celebration. When people from all over the Commonwealth gather together to celebrate a significant occasion for their Head of State, such events serve to further emphasize the Sovereign's function as a focal point for national identity and togetherness.

There were celebrations for The Queen's Silver Jubilee in 1977 all around the UK and Commonwealth.
Church services were held all month long to celebrate the actual anniversary of The Queen's Accession on February 6, 1952. The full jubilee celebrations got under way in the summer of 1977, and the Queen and her family spent the anniversary weekend at Windsor. The Queen was addressed by both Houses of Parliament on May 4 in the Palace of Westminster, and in her

response, she emphasized that the theme of the jubilee was to be the unity of the nation.

The Queen wanted to celebrate her jubilee by spending as much time as she could with her people, so she set off on a massive tour during the summer. The 36 counties that were covered by the six jubilee visits across the UK and Northern Ireland were more than any other Sovereign had ever visited in just three months. Glasgow experienced its busiest day ever when the home tours started there on May 17. The trips carried on throughout Wales and England.

In 2002, a jam-packed calendar of activities was held to commemorate The Queen's fifty years of rule. Celebration, Community, Service, Past and Future, Giving Thanks, and Commonwealth were six major Jubilee themes that influenced events.

A very busy year for the royal couple resulted from the Queen and The Duke of Edinburgh's extended tours of the Commonwealth and the UK.

The Queen celebrated her 80th birthday on June 17, 2006, after turning 80 on April 21, 2006. Numerous celebrations were held both on and around Her Majesty's real birthday, April 21, as well as on her formal birthday, June 17, to mark the occasion.

The magic of reading was celebrated at Buckingham Palace with a special Children's Party at the Palace. 2,000 kids were invited, and a theatrical performance including a cameo from The Queen was broadcast live on the BBC.

Her Majesty's formal birthday was celebrated at Trooping the Colour as it does every year, but this year there was a special flypast and "feu de joie" (fire of joy) to honour the event.

Thanksgiving services were held at St. George's Chapel in Windsor and St. Paul's Cathedral, with lunch being served at Mansion House in London after the latter. A "Service over sixty" reception held by Her Majesty honored guests over the age of sixty who have significantly contributed to national life, as did the Help the Aged Living Legends Awards at Windsor Castle. The Queen celebrated with other members of her generation who had similarly led a life of service and dedication. Additionally, visitors who shared her 80th birthday on April 19 were invited to Buckingham Palace. The Queen celebrated her actual birthday by strolling through Windsor and mingling with the populace. She then went to a special family luncheon at the recently rebuilt Kew Palace, which was followed by a grand fireworks show.

During her 80th birthday year, Her Majesty received about 40,000 birthday messages from the general people.

A spectacular central weekend and a number of regional tours across the UK and Commonwealth were held to commemorate the Diamond Jubilee.
While other members of the Royal Family traveled to every Commonwealth realm in 2012, The Queen and The Duke of Edinburgh visited every region of England, Scotland, Wales, and Northern Ireland. The Duke and Duchess of Cambridge traveled to Tuvalu, and The Prince of Wales and The Duchess of Cornwall visited Australia, Canada, New Zealand, and Papua New Guinea. The Queen's attendance at the Epsom Derby on Saturday marked the start of the key weekend. As part of the Diamond Jubilee celebrations, "Big Jubilee Lunches" were organized on Sunday throughout the UK. Building on the already well-liked "Big Lunch" concept, individuals were urged to enjoy lunch with neighbors and friends.
On Sunday, close to 1,000 vessels from the UK, the Commonwealth, and other countries gathered on the Thames for the Thames Diamond Jubilee Pageant. The Royal Barge, the centerpiece of the flotilla, carried The Queen and The Duke of Edinburgh. At a concert organized by Take That singer-songwriter Gary Barlow for the BBC on Monday to celebrate the Diamond Jubilee against the backdrop of Buckingham Palace, a number of well-known figures gathered. William, Stevie Wonder, Grace Jones, and Kylie Minogue were among the performers.

The National Beacon was one of 2,012 Beacons that were lighted by communities and people around the UK, Channel Islands, Isle of Man, and the Commonwealth after the concert. The Queen lit the National Beacon. A day of festivities in the heart of London marked the end of the Diamond Jubilee weekend. They began with a service at St. Paul's Cathedral, continued with two receptions, lunch at Westminster Hall, a carriage procession to Buckingham Palace, and ended with a balcony appearance, flypast, and fete de joie.

In order to accept gifts from anyone desiring to honor Her Majesty during her Diamond Jubilee year, the Queen's Diamond Jubilee Trust was established. The money donated has gone to programs like Queen's Young Leaders, which assists young people all over the Commonwealth who are breaking new ground in their neighborhoods.

The Queen became the monarch of Britain with the longest reign on September 9, 2015.

On April 21, 2016, the Queen turned 90, and on June 11, 2016, the second day of three days of national celebrations, she turned 90 officially.

Prior to presenting a plaque designating The Queen's Walkway, Her Majesty spent her actual birthday in Windsor, where she greeted well-wishers during a walkabout in the town center and others celebrating their 90th birthdays. In the late evening, Her Majesty and The Prince of Wales ignited the main beacon, which launched a chain of more than 900 beacons across the nation and around the world to commemorate her monumental achievement.

Until her demise, she has had a milestone of achievements which were not extensively analyzed in this book.

Chapter Five
British Royal History

Athelstan (895-939 AD), a member of the House of Wessex and the 30th great-grandunde of Queen Elizabeth II, was the first monarch of all of England. He was the descendant of Alfred the Great. Invading Vikings were finally driven out of Britain by the Anglo-Saxon ruler, who ruled from 925 to 939 AD. The kingship was transferred from the king to his firstborn son beginning with the reign of William the Conqueror. The Act of Settlement, passed by the British Parliament in 1702, altered this by stating that upon the death of King William III, the title or monarch would pass to Anne and the "heirs of her body." This meant that a woman might inherit the throne as long as there was no male heir to take her place. English common law at the time stipulated that male heirs received the kingdom before their sisters. The Act of Settlement also provided that any heir who married a Roman Catholic would be dropped from the line of succession, a recognition to the dominance of the Church of England. It wasn't until 2013 that Parliament passed the Succession to the Crown Act that the laws governing who could succeed to the British throne were once again amended. As a result, the kingdom would now pass to the first-born heir, regardless of gender, under an absolute primogeniture system of succession.

The king had the power to reject any unions within the royal family under the terms of the Royal Marriage Act of 1772. George III passed it in response to his ire over his younger brother Prince Henry's marriage to a commoner named Anne Horton.

Since then, royals who wanted to be married had to request permission from the Crown. This authorization wasn't always given. Famously, Queen Elizabeth II turned down Princess Margaret's wish to wed Peter Townsend because she deemed him unfit because he was a commoner and a divorcee. Peter Townsend was a military hero.

Prior to 2002, the Church of England did not let divorced persons to remarry, making getting a royal divorce a royal agony. Since the king simultaneously serves as the head of the Anglican Church, divorce and remarriage were practically outlawed for heirs to the throne. Ironic given that Henry VIII, after the Catholic Church refused to grant him an annulment from his first marriage to Catherine of Aragon, formed the church. Since the Royal Marriage Act of 1772 gave the king the ability to veto marriages within the royal family, any proposed match between royalty and a divorced individual was for centuries a non-starter due to the stigma surrounding divorce.

King George IV sought a divorce from Caroline of Brunswick, whom he charged with adultery, in front of a parliamentary tribunal in 1820. He merely succeeded in stirring up a scandal and underscoring the idea that you cannot simultaneously carry a crown and divorce papers.

In 1936, Edward VIII gave up his crown in order to wed American Wallis Simpson, who had previously been divorced twice. He was the last monarch who had to decide between succession and love. Princess Margaret, the sister of Queen Elizabeth II, was able to get a divorce in 1978 before the Church decision in 2002. Additionally, Princess Diana and Prince Charles' divorce was authorized by Elizabeth II in 1996. Later, Charles married the previously divorced Camilla Parker Bowles in 2005, and his son Harry later wed Meghan Markle in 2018.

Even though in a family where genes define authority, royal marriages to commoners began in the 15th century, they were never without controversy. Elizabeth Woodville was a widow who was secretly wedded by King Edward IV in 1464. The future King James II also wed Anne Hyde, a commoner with whom he had become pregnant but who died before he was crowned.

Following Prince Henry's union with commoner Anne Horton, the Royal Marriages Act of 1772 was enacted, thus ending royal-commoner unions for the next nearly 250 years. Royal weddings changed along with changes in society standards of union, divorce, and relationship. Prince William married Kate Middleton, whose parents run a party supply company, in 2011, while Prince Harry wed American actress Meghan Markle in 2018. Both of these royal children were given permission to wed commoners.

Conclusion

Without much ado, King Charles III, formerly Prince of Wales has already assumed the mantle of leadership after her mother's death; making him the oldest to have ascended the throne since the history of British Monarchy. His first son Prince Williams is apparently the heir presumptive.

Her mother was greatly revered and loved by all; a virtue which has consolidated the Commonwealth. With her death, many fear the continuation of this International body as King Charles III may likely not live up to expectations.

www.ingramcontent.com/pod-product-compliance
Lightning Source LLC
LaVergne TN
LVHW052112160826
845678LV00015B/3510

9798352836996